Talk To People!

25 Small Talk Conversation Starters To Relate And Talk To People Easily Using Communication Skills And Self Confidence Secrets!

Ryan Cooper

STOP!!! Before you read any further....Would you like to know the Secrets of Transforming your life, overcome insecurities, develop leadership skills, and undeniable confidence in your personal, professional, and relationship life?

If your answer is yes, then you are not alone. Thousands of people are looking for the secret to have unstoppable confidence and self-driven power in all areas of their lives.

If you have been searching for these answers without much luck, you're in the right place!

Not only will you gain incredible insight in this book, but because I want to make sure to give you as much value as possible, right now for a limited time you can get full **100% FREE access to a VIP bonus EBook** entitled **LIMITLESS ENERGY!**

Just Go Here For Free Instant Access:

www.PotentialRise.com

Legal Notice

Disclaimer Notice

Table Of Contents

Introduction

I want to thank you and congratulate you for purchasing the book, *"Talk To People! - 25 Small Talk Conversation Starters To Relate And Talk To People Easily Using Communication Skills And Self Confidence Secrets!"*.

This book on how to "Talk To People" contains proven steps and strategies on how to easily and quickly relate to people, overcome shyness and social anxiety, and make small talk with anyone!

In addition to providing you with all the proven steps and strategies on how to talk to people, this book also contains 25 small talk conversation starters that will have you self confident and ready to talk to anyone!

It is very easy to be the most charming and appealing person in a room. You may have secretly wanted to be that kind of person all your life – that type who could confidently chat with people you just know and influence them to make decisions with you. When you think about it, most of the actions that people do would actually say a lot about a person's life. Everything that you do is somewhat connected to the way people would relate to you. You can say what you want about yourself, but it would be your actions that would reveal your true self.

What you are about to read would be the most important and the simplest things that you have been wanting to learn. They will be all about how to fine tune your actions to make yourself feel and seem desirable and reliable. This book will help you make every sound that you make and any arbitrary action that you do draw others closer to you. After reading this book, you can expect to make more sales, get better contracts, or be able to make people believe in everything that you do or say.

Thanks again for purchasing this book, I hope you enjoy it!

Chapter 1: How To Talk To People By Relating To Them Quickly

You cannot avoid having a random conversation with someone you just met. In short, you cannot avoid making small talks. Your entire future may actually depend on it – you need to make conversations with an employer that you just met, or you need to make someone your acquaintance in order for you to land an opportunity.

The top 1% of the US population actually made their fortune first by making sure that they were able to make the best first impressions. Eventually, these people they just met funded their first project, became their business partners, or bought their ideas even before they became well-known entrepreneurs.

When you think about it, most of the opportunities that you get in life are not achieved entirely because of sheer luck. These opportunities are most likely based on your interactions with people who are bound to see your potential. The people who are going to give you a job may not be able to see what your skills are upon meeting you for the first time. However, they would still want to see if you are a person that they would like.

Hence, it is very important to make very interesting conversations to get other people to like you, even if you do not know where your future relationship with them would take you. It is because you would need to establish connections with anyone you would meet because sooner or later, they may do something that would benefit you.

Make People See That You Can Do Something for Them

The only reason why people would like to talk to you is because they find you interesting or, at the very least, worthy of their time. However, keep in mind that not everyone would actually want to spend time listening to you go on and on about yourself. To keep people interested in you, you have to make the conversation all about them. With this in mind, you would always remember to strike up conversations not about your ego, especially if you are expecting that other people can do so much for you.

Be That Person Who Would Initiate the Conversation

You may be very uncomfortable with this idea. After all, nobody would initially be that person who would want to jump into unknown territory and deal with the possibility of making a fool of himself. However, if you want something, you better have the stomach to pursue it.

Being able to start a conversation is a mark of a confident person. It is also an indication for others that you have what it takes to get what you want and that you are not hesitant to make others feel more important than you are. In addition, approaching another person for a chat would make them feel important.

People feel uneasy whenever someone they hardly know suddenly approaches them. They feel that the other person is after their money or trying to squeeze information out of them. If you make it obvious that you are interested in the other person but you are not willing to give them something that they can exploit, you would definitely get brushed off. You would just appear as a selfish person. Thus, make sure that if you are going to approach someone with a conversation starter, make them believe that you are going to give them something worth their time.

Chapter 2: Strategies For Communication Skills And Starting Conversations

Body language reveals a lot about the person even before you start talking to him. Studying how a person's face breaks into a smile, or quiver, or how he uses his hands will tell you about his personality even without knowing where he works or what his parents did for a living. The same rule applies when you start a conversation: whenever you start a conversation with someone else, your body language should go well with your words.

Listed below are 5 tips that could help you practice the right body language and thus allow you to instantly connect with people such as your future boss or your potential romantic partner.

1. Smile differently.

Smiling is the universal pleasant conversation starter. However, not all smiles are the same. There are certain smiles that would make people feel that you are not being sincere. If people see you smile way too much, that's a dead giveaway that you are being pretentious.

Your smile is one of the first impressions that you leave on a person, especially if you are trying to start a conversation. The most sincere smiles are those that are made slowly. Imagine yourself sitting at a poker table, and if you see someone whose lips are slowly forming an upward curve, you can almost guess that he has a good hand. That kind of smile is more convincing, and it reveals that you are genuinely interested in the other person.

2. Have good eye contact.

Eye contact is one of the initial gauges of people when it comes to knowing more about a person's sincerity. As a rule, people who avoid eye contact and who tend to randomly gaze at objects in a room would be considered uninterested in the topic of the conversation. Worse, they may be thought to be lying.

Establishing eye contact with the person that you are talking to is also a proven way to make him your friend, or at least get him very interested in you. It is proven that when you look like you are not distracted by anything else in the room and you are just paying attention to the face and the body language of the person you are talking to, he would build a certain level of trust and fondness towards you.

3. Face the other person fully.

Remember that when you were a child, you would easily know if your mom was giving you her full attention? People would still have that instinct to know if they are getting all the attention that they need at the moment. They would know when they are really welcome to join in the conversation. That is the moment when you fully face them, and flash them a wide smile.

Ladies, if you are wondering what would really attract men and make them engage in an animated conversation with you, this is the trick. You do not have to do or say anything else – just face them fully and flash them a wide smile. People who would tend to give half smiles and just look at others by tilting their head to the side would give mixed signals that they merely recognize the other person's presence but are not really interested to mingle. Pivoting right into the direction of the other person sends him the message "I really think you have something special."

4. Don't slouch.

If you are trying to make the impression that you are a winner and worthy of other people's attention, remember to watch your posture. Slouching is definitely a sign of being uninterested or feeling low, which is a far cry from the impression that you are trying to create. At the same time, slouching would somehow make you feel that you lack confidence. You won't see any successful man with poor posture, unless he has a health condition.

You may observe how slouching or having a straight back affects your mood. Whenever you slouch, you tend to feel that you cannot do anything right, or you feel a bit sleepy or uninterested in any person in the room. Sitting or standing straight, however, forces you to pay attention and it provides you a positive and

uplifting sensation. See how posture can affect your emotions? Make sure that you can impress people by emanating a positive attitude and confidence when you walk into a room.

5. Look intelligent using your eyes.

Now, here's another thing that you can do with your eyes – maintaining intense eye contact would allow you to look insightful, and would actually help you to think that you are that way. You may have tried doing so whenever you are really interested in the topic or the person that you are talking to. However, apart from conveying the message of interest, it also tells the other person that you are willing to join in the conversation.

A lot of men do this whenever they meet women that they like. They try to take in the most information that they can get by observing all the features that the woman possesses. In such a way, they are actually being intelligent. They are getting as much information as they can which is much more effective than simply getting cocky and jumping in with a pickup line that she's probably heard a dozen times already. Doing so allows men to make the right impression, and the ladies love it, especially if these men are good-looking.

There is something about a steady gaze that makes it effective. It is the feeling that the other person is attractive, and of course, everybody craves for that sensation.

When you think about it, these 5 tricks are the most effective ways to make sure that you are establishing the right connection with the people you want to talk to. Not only will these tricks allow you to make an instant good impression, they will also allow you to direct the conversation to where you would want it to go and captivate your audience.

Chapter 3: How To Stop Social Anxiety And Self Doubt Fast

Here's the part that you may not really like – after catching all the attention with your great body language, it's time to make the real interaction. Yes, that means that you have to initiate a small talk to keep the fire burning.

Not a lot of people like these talks because they think that these are a waste of everyone's time. However, it is very important to keep in mind that if you want to establish a connection with someone, you cannot always wait for the other person to approach you and engage you in a deep and meaningful conversation. Your relationship must start with something, even if it is out of something as mundane as "You come here often?"

Introducing Yourself Gives You the Upper Hand

In the first chapter, you read about your obligation of starting the conversation. That is not plainly to save the other person from the awkwardness of approaching a total stranger. Instead, think of it this way – starting the conversation gives you the benefit of being in control of how things would proceed later on.

You would want to establish that you are influential and you are someone important who is actually willing to give that other person your full attention. You are not likely to get something very fruitful, such as a sale or a signed contract, today. However, starting the conversation would allow you to establish that friendship that you want to build. Most of the time, other people wouldn't know that you want that to happen despite all the gestures that you make. You have to be firm and take the first step to get what you want.

True enough, you will get what you want when you say the right opening lines. You also allow yourself the time to study that other person to figure out what kind of conversation starters would most likely work on him. You would find that you get a kick out of knowing that other person more than revealing a lot about yourself. That is because you are getting a picture of what the connection between the two of you would look like in the future without jumping the gun and saying outright that you want a more formal relationship.

Reinforcing your Self-Esteem

Whenever you feel anxious during a conversation, it automatically shows. Your voice stammers, your hand quivers, and you instantly run out of things to say. Why do you feel that anxiety? It is because you feel that you are making a fool of yourself and you think that sooner or later, you will make a mess. That is why you get too conscious.

The quickest way to get away out of anxiety is to imagine that you are not being watched. People you talk to would more likely be paying attention to themselves and they would have the same worries as you do. It is natural, so don't make a big deal out of the situation. You know that once you find the sweet spot of the conversation, it will just flow.

At the same time, think that you can become impressive without even trying to. Act naturally – talk about things that you are comfortable discussing. In any case, you feel that you should give the other person the airtime, ask him about the things that interest him. That would put the spotlight on him, but he would not mind. Everybody wants to talk about themselves; they are just too shy to admit it. That would allow you to get more information from the other person and at the same time feel comfortable that you are establishing the connection.

Remember that conversations should not be all about you. Once you feel that you are making the other person want to talk more, you will feel less awkward.

Practice Makes It Easier for You

When it comes to meeting and talking to strangers, it still holds true that practice makes perfect. The more you strike up conversations with people you do not know, the more you feel that you are capable of talking to people whom you think are more important than you. It is because you are now allowing yourself to be exposed to different types of people, and it makes you a lot more "people-smart." That means that you would be able to identify different traits and the best corresponding approach to a number of personality types. Now, you are ready to establish connections with people who used to intimidate you. If you want to be part of the society's inner circle, take time to practice.

Chapter 4: Keeping The Conversation Going

There is nothing more frustrating than not being able to get into a group or to make the other person you want to talk to ease up on you. People are often judgmental, and it is natural for people to feel distrust towards strangers. It is part of most people's upbringing to not talk to strangers. However, it is also because they do not have encounters with a lot of people that would make them feel comfortable about themselves. Nobody wants to be put out of their comfort zone. However, with the right skills and knowhow, you will have the ability to be placed out of the box.

You may sometimes feel that you are losing your confidence whenever another person dismisses you. However, do not feel dissuaded. You must have done something wrong. Not a lot of people would actually allow you to just butt in if they're engaged in something important. You must learn to take things slowly. If you want to approach a group, make it a point that you show interest in the main speaker. Keep your distance but make sure that they see you. Your genuine interest will make them feel that it is necessary to invite you in their group.

Once you are in, make it a point that you listen to them first. Observe their body language and listen to how these people speak to each other. Without making a move yet, come up with a strategy. Pay attention to their body language; that would show you a lot about their personality. Wait for them to show you some signs that they believe that you are welcome in their group; then you can start talking. Doing all the tips in the previous chapter would actually speed up this process.

Make Them Lead the Talk

Here's a good thing that you should remember, especially if you know that you feel hesitant about talking a lot to a group of strangers: these people like to talk. They like to talk about the things that they know, their accomplishments, their dreams. They want to engage in conversations that would make them feel good about themselves. That is what you should give them.

Here's the key to making conversations last the entire night: ask a lot of open-ended questions. Make sure that you just don't ask them where they work; ask them what they do for a living. Ask them what their parents are like. Ask them what they think about the party or about politics. That would keep them talking all night about themselves. That would make them feel happy.

Use Enthusiasm

When you feel that they are talking about something that they are passionate about, make sure your emotion matches theirs. Use enthusiasm to reinforce their positive emotion. That would surely make them feel that you understand their feelings and that you look at things the same way.

Matching their enthusiasm about things would not only make them feel happy about themselves. That would also make them feel that they should be honored to match your enthusiasm about what you will talk about later in the conversation. That would make it a lot easier for you to invite another person to another engagement the next time.

Say Your Name and Ask For Theirs

A person who does not ask people their names is more likely not really interested in them. A person's name is the most important word for them. It's the first thing that they learned about themselves, and it is how they will know that you really paid attention to all the things that they said and that you are looking forward to meeting them again.

Asking for another person's name is easy. However, it would be a challenging for them to remember yours. For that reason, here's a trick that you should remember: Whenever you introduce yourself, say your name twice. For example, you can say "I'm Bruce. Bruce Wayne," or "I'm Bruce Wayne, but you can call me Bruce."

Make sure that you use the other person's name throughout the conversation; that will be music to their ears, and they will feel obligated to return the favor. If you want them to reach you after your initial engagement, you can give him your business card, but make sure that you ask for his card first. Asking the other person's card is also a sure way that you would remember their name, and it would not be awkward to ask for their name again.

Should You Ask Them To Do Something For You?

This is something that you would probably ask yourself if you are a salesperson or if you are in a business engagement and you need some people to listen to your pitch or ideas: it will be okay to do so after you have listened to them first. Alternatively, you can feel that it is okay to talk to people about what you do for a living once you can sense that there are a lot of things in common between you.

However, keep in mind that there is no one out there who would actually want to hear what you have to sell before you established that you are their friend. So make sure that they feel at ease with you before you talk about whatever it is you're selling.

Chapter 5: Self Confidence Secrets And How To Overcome Shyness

You can't help it – there will be times when you would feel that you are too awkward to talk to people, or that you would feel unwelcome. However, remember that there is a simpler way to make people like you, even if you are the outsider in the group. You just need to be yourself and make them aware that the best part of your personality is that you would always want to provide others what they need first.

Remember that you are not merely trying to be impressive; you are already impressive in your own way. You do not have to be someone that you are not. Simply show other people the best side of you and you would be alright.

Watch Your Posture

Your posture is a dead giveaway of how you are feeling. When you are scared of talking to other people, your posture stoops and then you would not be able to smile. However, your body reacts to your emotions and your emotions would also react to your body. If you feel that you do not have an ounce of charisma in you or if you feel that you are losing your confidence, fix your posture. Curve your lips slowly into a smile and you would feel a lot better to yourself. This trick would actually work when you feel that you are having a bad hair day or feeling nervous right before a job interview.

Think About Good Things

If you are still wondering whether or not you should talk to people, think about all the random conversations that you made with other people in the past. That would remind you that you have talked to a lot of strangers before, and most of the time, those conversations turned out okay. Just remember that if you have done it once, you can always do it again, and you would do even better.

However, if you are really nervous about starting conversations, think about all the benefits that you get out of small talks whether you started them or not. You would find that you actually would feel good after those conversations, and that you survived them before. You can also ask a friend to help you practice.

Just remember that you do not have to be conscious since other people are not really paying that much attention to you. They are probably even more self-conscious than you are. That is why the sure-fire way to gain new friends is to actually make them talk about the things that make them feel great. Putting the spotlight on them is a great way to make them feel at ease, and make yourself feel confident that no one is really minding the way you look or talk.

Making the Graceful Exit

Good exits are tricky to master, especially if you ended up talking to a group of people who would not seem to stop talking and you are really feeling out of place or you would actually want to talk to other people. The main reason why people get "trapped" in a conversation is they do not want their new acquaintance to feel rejected or offended by their abrupt departure.

Here's the trick: mix your parting statement with a compliment or two. You can say something like "I'm terribly sorry. I remembered that I have to catch this person before he leaves, but that was a really great conversation about the importance of lime juice in our daily activities. I'm really glad to have discussed this with you as you are very knowledgeable in this field."

What happens next is that the other person would be grateful for your compliment and would not keep you in their company any longer. Notice that you would not really need to lie about why you want to leave the conversation. That is much better than saying "Oh, look at the time!" or "I need to use the bathroom." It would be really awkward for both of you if you bump into each other in the next room with you engaged in a conversation with another person.

Chapter 6: 25 Conversation Starters To Easily Talk To Anyone!

Having trouble thinking of what to say first to that person you want to talk to? Do you typically wonder what topics would probably break the ice? Don't worry; it happens to everyone. To help you, here are some conversation starters that you could use to warm up to a person or a crowd. Just fill in the blanks in order for your chosen starter to be appropriate for the occasion:

1. That's a really nice _____. Where did you get it?

Make someone talk about their most remarkable acquisition. More often than not, there is a good story behind the stuff that they own, and they would not mind telling it.

2. What do you think about this place/party?

Ask a person about the location that you have in common. That would allow you to express your opinion about an event that you are both familiar with. Alternately, you can also ask about how they are related or connected to the people who invited you.

3. It must be _____ to have a _____.

Look at their neutral physical traits. You can ask a left-handed person if it is harder to write with their left hand, and they will say that it has its merits. Look for their characteristics that would potentially give them a lot of credit. A guitarist would really love to talk about how he or she performs.

4. What got you into _____?

Talk to people about their job or their hobby as they would feel good tracing their beginnings. After that, compliment them for their hard work.

5. Would you be able to tell if a _____ is _____?

Observe what a person would probably do best or if something is within his skill set, then ask his opinion as an expert.

6. Why do you think your company is _____?

You can immediately sense a person's opinion about his job or the place that he is working for. Make him voice out his thoughts.

7. What is your favorite time of the year?

Everybody would like to talk about their personal holidays. Give them that opportunity.

8. What can you say about the food?

You would definitely want to find out what someone likes to eat. In any case, you would want to invite that person out.

9. If you would choose your name, what would it be?

Name change reveals a lot about someone's personality. That would be interesting.

10. Would you want to live in another place?

Locations also reveal a lot about someone's personality. These opinions reveal what he thinks about the opportunities that exist in his chosen area.

11. What can you say about the weather we've been having lately?

This is one of the first things that anyone would ask someone. There is a good reason why it works.

12. What got you interested in _____?

Asking this question would reveal how a person acquired and developed his expertise. It would also reveal possible mentors and possible contacts.

13. What makes your job hard?

People stay in their jobs because it is challenging. That would make them talk about what made them the expert in their field.

14. What's the most interesting thing that happened at work?

You would know how a person feels about life in general if you would ask what he would find amusing in an activity that he does every day.

15. I see that you _____. What other _____ do you _____?

There are a lot of blanks there, but this line of inquiry is applicable to a lot of people. For example, you can ask a musician about what other instruments he or she can play.

16. What made you choose _____?

It could be a school, a company, or a product. Whatever a person chooses always has a good story behind it.

17. How do you know _____?

Ask people about their relationships with another person. That would tell you how they are connected with your existing contacts.

18. What do you think would happen 5 years from now?

You can ask this in line with the other person's belief about the economy or about everything that is happening around him. That would make you know what relationship you would have with that person in the future.

19. Tell me about your most absurd experience in _____.

The most absurd experience in the event that both of you are familiar with would reveal a lot about your similarities and differences. This would give you an idea of what the other person would regard as strange.

20. How did you _____?

Asking someone about his methods would make you see that there are hidden skills other than the ones that he uses in his line of work. That would tell you other things that this person can offer you.

21. How do you think this problem can be solved?

Make a person solve a common problem and avoid seeming like a know-it-all. That would make you likable.

22. What is it like to be the _____?

Pay the other person a nice compliment by making it seem like his entire line of expertise is a very good thing. That would make him feel great for being himself and then make him want to talk more about his assets.

23. What changes happened ever since you joined/became _____?

People believe that they can make improvements the moment they step in an endeavor. That is something worth hearing about.

24. How did you make that happen?

Ask the person about the most important thing that he has done for someone else. Then ask him how he made it happen.

25. Do you believe in _____?

This might be a gray area, but you would want to know more about the values the other person adheres to.

Conclusion

Thank you again for purchasing this book on how to talk to people!

I am extremely excited to pass this information along to you, and I am so happy that you now have read and can hopefully implement these strategies going forward.

I hope this book was able to help you understand the easy to implement methods of making small talk and meeting people.

The next step is to get started using this information to begin conversing with all walks of people and lead a much more fulfilling life!

Please don't be someone who just reads this information and doesn't apply it, the strategies in this book will only benefit you if you use them!

If you know of anyone else that could benefit from the information presented here please inform them of this book.

Finally, if you enjoyed this book and feel it has added value to your life in any way, please take the time to share your thoughts and post a review on Amazon. It'd be greatly appreciated!

Thank you and good luck!

Preview Of:

The Ultimate Guide To:

<u>Self Confidence!</u>

Stop Shyness And Self Doubt, Develop Great Social Skills, Build Charisma, And Begin Feeling Good About Yourself!

Introduction

I want to thank you and congratulate you for purchasing the book, *"Self Confidence: The Ultimate Guide To Self Confidence! - Stop Shyness And Self Doubt, Develop Great Social Skills, Build Charisma, And Begin Feeling Good About Yourself"*

This "Self Confidence" book contains proven steps and strategies on how to Stop Shyness and Self Doubt for good!

This ultimate guide to self confidence is an easy to implement guide with proven steps and strategies to build self confidence and charisma and to begin feeling good about yourself!

It is aimed to help you overcome your social anxieties; free yourself from the bondage of self-doubt; and unleash the confidence in you. Confidence is what fuels the person to move forward. It is the driving force that enables us to overcome any inhibitions that may hinder our progress.

Confident people are attractive. They are usually more successful in life than those who prefer to work in the sidelines. If you are confident, you can be who you want to be and you can achieve whatever your goals are. It will be possible with the help of this eBook.

Success is just around the corner. If you are confident, you will be able to chase your dreams without second guessing yourself, and start actually living your dreams instead of sitting on the sidelines. Be free. Be socially skilled...Be popular...

Be confident and go to greater heights...

Thanks again for purchasing this book, I hope you enjoy it!

Chapter 1: Self-Confidence And Its Importance*

Imagine a room full of people and suddenly a confident person walks in, what do you think will happen? If that person were to speak, do you think everyone would listen? Does a confident person give up easily when assigned with a difficult task? Does he run into a corner at the first sight of failure?

Confident people get the attention of everyone when they enter a room full of people. When they speak, everyone listens. When they are assigned with a difficult task, they don't give up easily and instead they are grateful to be given the opportunity to showcase their talents. When they think they are about to fail, confident people moves forward and say "Bring it on or I can do this!"

Self-confidence is a trait that everyone wants to have but only a few will be able to get.

So, how do we define self-confidence? When you know what you are capable of, you take pride in your own value as a person, and when you are able to convey that to others, that is self-confidence. Arrogance is not self-confidence for it is when you have an unrealistic view of yourself; you think you are better than you actually are. In contrast, when you think that you are less valuable than others, you have a low self-esteem.

So why is self-confidence important?

Before we enumerate the importance of self-confidence, it is imperative for us to define our goals first. You have to know what you are aiming for. Otherwise, developing self-confidence will only lead you nowhere than where you have started.

Here are some of the reasons why self-confidence is important:

1. **Confidence is an effective ingredient in**

relationships: There are lots of researchers who believe that confidence is more important than good looks when it comes to relationships. Men and women find confidence as an attractive trait to the opposite sex. A confident woman walks in and men start tailing her. Similarly, a confident smile to a woman can capture her attention. Confidence is not only important in the dating phase of the relationship. Couples who are both confident in themselves and in the relationship are more likely to last than those who are overshadowed by their partner.

2. **Confidence leads to career growth**: Confident people naturally do well in everything. Even when they fail, they think that they at least know what they need to do to succeed next time. This type of mentality often attracts growth and promotion at work. When you believe in your abilities as a sales person, and when you believe in the product you sell, there is a greater chance that you surpass the required quota for sales and that definitely is an accomplishment. Studies have also shown that people who started developing confidence earlier in life are more likely to succeed than those who were only taught to aim for higher standards.

3. **Confidence gains people's trust**: Confidence breeds trust. People who are confident about their skills and talents are trusted by their colleagues to finish the job, and do it well. They are trusted by their classmates to win a contest on behalf of their class. Confident people are trusted by the people around them to excel in any field they choose to take. Although it may be a little burdensome, the trust that people give can somehow make a confident person strive harder and achieve what he is intended to accomplish; actually making him more confident in the process.

4. **Confidence defines how we live our life**: If you are a person who always want to be alone and work in the sidelines, and if you don't feel good about yourself because you believe you're not good enough, you are most probably living a miserable life. If you are confident with whom you are, people will be drawn to you regardless of your outward appearance. When you enjoy being with people, you get to

enjoy life and everything it offers.

5. **Confidence helps us to communicate better and get what we want in life:** If you are confident, you are not afraid to say what you want. You are capable of saying no when you need to, and people will always value your opinions. Learning to say what you want can make a big impact in your life. Express yourself honestly and appropriately will definitely get you what you want in life.

Thanks for Previewing My Exciting Book Entitled:

"Self Confidence: Stop Shyness And Self Doubt, Develop Great Social Skills, Build Charisma, And Begin Feeling Good About Yourself!"

To purchase this book, simply go to the Amazon Kindle store and simply search:

"SELF CONFIDENCE"

Then just scroll down until you see my book. You will know it is mine because you will see my name "Ryan Cooper" underneath the title.

Alternatively, you can visit my author page on Amazon to see this book and other work I have done. Thanks so much, and please don't forget your free bonuses

DON'T LEAVE YET! - CHECK OUT YOUR FREE BONUSES BELOW!

Free Bonus Offer: Get Free Access To The PotentialRise.com VIP Newsletter!

Once you enter your email address you will immediately get free access to this awesome newsletter!

But wait, right now if you join now for free you will also get free access to the "LIMITLESS ENERGY" free EBook!

To claim both your FREE VIP NEWSLETTER MEMBERSHIP and your FREE BONUS Ebook on LIMITLESS ENERGY!

Just Go To:

www.PotentialRise.com